PICKUP

TRUCKS

BY
Michael Benson

PHOTOS BY BARRY C. ALTMARK

Crescent Books

New York • Avenel

ACKNOWLEDGMENTS

The author wishes to acknowledge the following persons and organizations, without whose help this book would have been impossible. Lisa and Tekla Benson, Frank Calderon, Maria Damiani, Nancy Davis, Rita Eisenstein, Dave Grayson, David Henry Jacobs, Norman Jacobs, Katharine Repole, Milburn Smith, Jose Soto.

Unless otherwise noted, all photos are by Barry C. Altmark.

Published by Crescent Books,
distributed by Random House Value Publishing, Inc.
40 Engelhard Avenue, Avenel, New Jersey 07001.

Library of Congress Cataloging-in-Publication Data

Benson, Michael.
    Pickup trucks / by Michael Benson ; photos by Barry C. Altmark
        p. cm.
    Includes index.
    ISBN 0-517-14689-4
    1. Trucks—History.   I. Title
TL230.B385 1995   95-14780
629.223— dc20   CIP

Printed and bound in China

10 9 8 7 6 5 4 3 2 1

CONTENTS

Introduction
PICKUPS

MEAN FREEDOM

At the turn of the century, the automobile replaced the horse as the primary power behind land travel. Therefore, it isn't surprising that the motor vehicle soon was called upon to replace the horse-drawn cart as the number-one method of hauling things from one place to another.

The 1990 Chevy 454 SS pickup was a full-sized pickup. The model was first introduced in 1936 and by 1990 was selling more than a half a million units a year. The truck came in either two- or four-wheel drive and both versions came with either a six-and-a-half-foot box or an eight-foot box. Trucks like the one shown here were produced at the General Motors plant in Fort Wayne, Indiana; Pontiac, Michigan; and Oshawa, Ontario.

Thus was born the pickup truck—a modified car with a big box in the back and enough strength to get the goods from the farm to the market. The pickup truck was quickly woven into the fabric of American life, a symbol of freedom, of successful small business, of rural pride. The pickup truck was the American Dream for the self-employed everywhere, but especially for the workers of God's good American earth.

Use your imagination

The pickup truck can do a lot more than just haul. Any pickup owner will tell you that his truck is functional in a thousand ways. During its history, the pickup has found itself playing many odd and unintended roles.

Park the pickup next to the skinny-dipping hole and you've got yourself a sundeck. Lower the tailgate and you've got a diving board.

PREVIOUS PAGE: In 1990, the Chevrolet S-10 pickup came with either two- or four-wheel drive—and each was available with either a six-foot or a seven-and-a-half-foot box.

On many an occasion, a pickup has served admirably as a makeshift bandstand.

Of course, pickups are perfect for hunters. Not only do they have a natural spot to mount the gun rack, but they make it easy to get the buck home.

Bust up a few bales in the back and its a hayride. Anyone who's ever hitchhiked out in the country can tell you what a butt-breaking experience it can be to, "Climb in the back."

In the fifties and sixties when Drive-In movies were the rage, pickup trucks were some of the few vehicles that routinely parked backwards in the open-air theaters.

Hey, why do you think they call it a bed?

Loving tribute

So here is our loving tribute to the good ol' pickup truck. You'll read a complete history of the pickup,

from the Model C's of 1905 to today's Ford Ranger.

We'll show you and tell you about some of the more exciting things that people do with their pickup trucks—like taking them out to the local racetrack, customizing them, or metamorphozing them into monster trucks.

And throughout you'll be enjoying the great photography of Barry C. Altmark, the Associate Editor of Stock Car Spectacular magazine. He will not only show you shiny pickups, freshly waxed and posed in front of a scenic backdrop. He'll show you how pickup trucks really look, too—lovable and maybe a little muddy, a few two by fours sticking up out of the box.

—Michael Benson

The 1990 Chevy Short Bed pickup sacrificed some room in the box, but compensated for it by making room inside the cab for a driver and four passengers.

The 1951 Ford truck could have been the ugliest pickup in automotive history. Gone were the horizontal grille bars of the previous year, and in their place was this gaping mouth with three horrible teeth (or five if you counted the headlights which were mounted to the ends of the dental stucture). The protrusions were called "Dagmars," after the buxom TV personality.

A HISTORY OF PICKUP TRUCKS

A year-by-year guide

1905

The first commercially produced pickup truck was the Delivery Car, manufactured by the Ford Motor Company. Ford's Model C car was simply fitted to a delivery body.

The wheelbase measured 78 inches. Only ten of the vehicles were produced, costing customers about $950 each. The two-cylinder, 120.5 cubic inch (ci) engine with a two-speed transmission produced ten horsepower (hp).

The experiment only lasted for one year before production was stopped—but the concept had taken hold. For the next several years many Ford cars were independently converted into pickups.

The need for a cargo-hauling vehicle was there.

1912

Ford brought the Delivery Car back. If other people were going to make pickups out of their cars anyway, Ford figured that they might as well do it themselves.

The new Delivery Cars looked about the same as the old ones. The same 1905 Model C body was used. But under the hood there was more than twice as much power as there had been seven years before.

A four-cylinder, 176.7 ci engine now produced 22 hp. Backed by an ad campaign that promised Delivery Cars to be "stronger than an army mule and cheaper than a team of horses," more than 17,000 were made.

Cost: About $650.

The Delivery Car proved to be of such lasting popularity that it was continually produced yet remained basically unchanged until 1925.

1918

Chevrolet began to cater to the truck market. Although it would be more than ten years before Chevy would market a full-fledged pickup truck, they did offer two car chassis with only a cowl, a hood and front fenders. Buyers would then attach their own truck body, which of course had to come from another manufacturer.

The two chassis were: 1) the 490 Commercial, the lighter of the two, a half-ton truck with a 102-inch

This 1966 Chevy has a big 350 ci powerplant under its hood!

The Dodge Ram 350 Heavy Duty pickup was equipped with a Cummins Turbo Diesel engine. It was so heavy-duty that four wheels weren't enough. It had a double axle in the rear and ran on six wheels!

wheelbase, and 2) the Model T, a full-ton truck, which came with the engine and transmission of the Chevy FA series included.

(Yes, despite the fact that Ford had been calling their most popular car the Model T since 1909, Chevy used the name for their new truck anyway. Things sure have changed.)

Buying just the chassis of a truck made sense to a lot of buyers, as they could buy a customized body or, if their old truck's body was still in good shape, they could move it onto their new chassis.

The 490 Commercial had a great cargo capacity despite its weight because of heavier springs in the suspension. The Model T came with a seat, but a cab still had to be fitted over it. The Model T came with adequate pulling power because it had a low-reduction worm drive differential, rather than the ring-and-pinion rear end that was standard in Chevy cars at the time.

The worm drive meant lower maximum speeds but no one seemed to mind. In 1918, total sales for the two truck chassis was 879. The following year that figure ballooned to more than 8,000.

1921

By 1921, Chevy correctly assumed that they could sell more truck chassis if they offered a chassis with a body

already attached. Since Chevrolet still didn't manufacture truck bodies, they cut deals with other manufacturers to deliver their bodies to Chevy's plants. The bodies were then attached to the chassis and sold as one piece. The Chevys didn't have to become pickup trucks. Since almost any body would fit on the Chevy chassis, some people preferred to turn their chassis into an enclosed delivery wagon. Some of the chassis were even transformed into fire trucks.

Also in 1921, Chevy added a third chassis option for potential truck owners. The new chassis, the Model G, was identical to the 490, except for additional room in the cargo area. The Model G had a 120-inch wheelbase.

1925

In addition to the Delivery Car, which was now in its last year of production, Ford introduced a new pickup, the Model T Pickup. The truck was a simply modified Model T roadster with a small cargo box replacing the turtle deck in the rear. Almost 150,000 were made at a cost to consumers of $281 apiece. The following year, Chevrolet finally manufactured its first pickup, attaching a cargo box to the truck of either a coupe or roadster.

A 1990 Dodge Ram.

The 1986 Chevrolet Custom Deluxe.

The 1947 Advanced Design models were the first newly designed Chevy trucks since the outbreak of World War II. Though civilian production of trucks resumed for Chevrolet immediately after the victory in the Pacific over the Japanese, those early post-war trucks were identical to pre-war models.

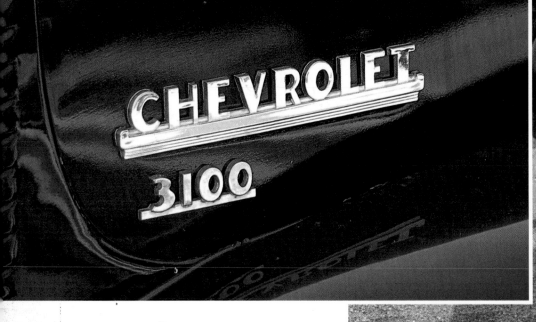

1928

Ford's Model T had been replaced by the Model A as its number one passenger car. Therefore, in 1928, the new truck from Ford was called the Model A Pickup. The Model A, in all of its incarnations, car and truck, is notable because it may have been the most durable motor vehicle ever produced. Astoundingly, out of the more than four million Model A's manufactured by Ford, more than a million are still in existence, still running—and it's now 67 years later!

The truck, available in either the roadster or closed-cab models, had a metal box attached to the kick panel on the passenger side for holding small items, a precursor to the glove compartment, and especially helpful in a vehicle being used to operate a business. The truck had three-speed sliding gear transmission and four-wheel mechanical brakes. The engine produced 40 hp.

The 1947 Chevrolet 3100 pickup. When designing the tailgate for these trucks, Chevy wanted to make sure that everyone knew who the manufacturer was.

In 1947 Chevrolet introduced their Advanced Design Series of pickups, and today these trucks remain a favorite among collectors.

The 1989 Dodge Dakota. Though smaller than a full-sized truck, the Dakota can still sit three grown men in the front seat.

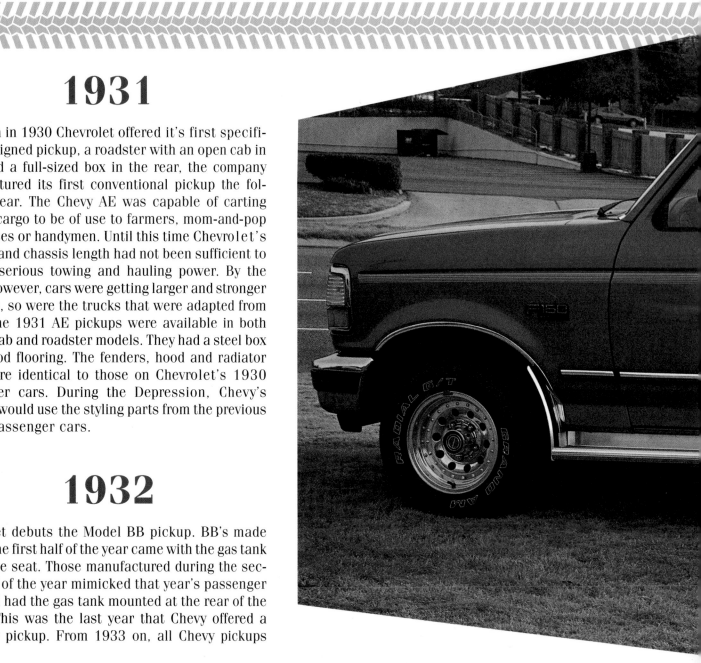

1931

Although in 1930 Chevrolet offered it's first specifically designed pickup, a roadster with an open cab in front and a full-sized box in the rear, the company manufactured its first conventional pickup the following year. The Chevy AE was capable of carting enough cargo to be of use to farmers, mom-and-pop businesses or handymen. Until this time Chevrolet's engines and chassis length had not been sufficient to provide serious towing and hauling power. By the 1930s however, cars were getting larger and stronger and thus, so were the trucks that were adapted from them. The 1931 AE pickups were available in both closed-cab and roadster models. They had a steel box with wood flooring. The fenders, hood and radiator shell were identical to those on Chevrolet's 1930 passenger cars. During the Depression, Chevy's pickups would use the styling parts from the previous year's passenger cars.

1932

Chevrolet debuts the Model BB pickup. BB's made during the first half of the year came with the gas tank under the seat. Those manufactured during the second half of the year mimicked that year's passenger cars and had the gas tank mounted at the rear of the frame. This was the last year that Chevy offered a roadster pickup. From 1933 on, all Chevy pickups

Ford's F-series continues to be the most popular pickup in America. Perhaps this was because they were one of the first manufacturers to realize that between a quarter and a third of all new pickup buyers are women. Here's a 1992 F-150 with its camper shell on.

With the camper shell on, the 1992 Ford F-150 resembles an overgrown station wagon. This is intentional, as it was designed to be useful and appealing to families.

were closed-cab. Chevy trucks outmuscled Chevy's cars slightly, 53 hp to 50 hp.

The 1932 Ford Model B Pickup became the first low-priced motor vehicle (i.e. not a racer) to come with a 65-hp V-8 engine. The new V-8 went into production late in 1932, so only the last few trucks to come off the assembly line that year have it. Those produced earlier in the year came equipped with a four-cylinder, 50-hp engine.

The Model B truck, available as a roadster or a closed-cab, was ten inches longer than the Model A, and had larger headlights and a larger cargo box. The front grille now sported vertical ribs and was shaped like a shield.

1933

Chevy pickups now sported a support brace bolted to their radiator shell. This allowed the headlamp support bar, radiator and front fenders to be bolted into

A 1987 Jeep Comanche equipped with a chrome tool box.

By the time Ford made this F-150 in 1986, they had been building the model for 13 years.

The F-150 model was originally manufactured by Ford because it was exempt from catalytic converter requirements. Standard for the F-150 was a 300 ci six-cylinder engine.

No one will ignore this 1966 Chevrolet Custom Deluxe, although the lavender paint job may not suit everyone's taste.

a single assembly. The improvement, called by the Chevy marketing department "stabilized unit mounting," offered the new trucks greater rigidity in the front assembly. The 206 ci engine could produce 65 hp. For the first time, Chevy pickups came with a four-speed transmission option. The standard color was Blue Bell Blue. Non-standard colors included black, brown, tan, gray, dark blue, maroon, red orange and yellow.

The 1933 Ford Model B Pickup looked very much the same as the 1932 model, but the wheelbase had grown to 112 inches. The V-8 engine was produced for the entire year, although the four-cylinder engine was still optional. The 1933 V-8 engine was Ford's strongest yet in a commercial vehicle, pumping out 75 hp.

1934

With its canted windshield pillar, arched cab roof and its streamlined (well, less box-like) body, the 1934 Chevy BB was a lot snazzier looking than its predecessors. And it was tougher, too. For the first time Chevrolet produced sheet metal specifically for their pickups. Until this time the trucks had used sheet metal designed for passenger cars.

The deluxe model or Chevy DB, had the engine moved forward on the frame. This, along with a longer 112-inch wheelbase, meant that there was more load space than ever. The DBs came with an optional canopy to cover the box, in case you were hauling something that shouldn't get wet.

Ford's 1934 pickups were identical in appearance to the 1933 models, but in this year Ford offered only one engine, the 221 ci flathead V-8. Mostly closed-cab

trucks were made. You could still order a roadster, but only 347 people did.

1935

New styling improved the 1935 Ford pickup. The cab had a sleeker shape, there was a canted windshield and the radiator grille was shaped like a V. The cab sat further back on the frame and the doors reached down to the floorboards, eliminating the awkward step-over the driver formerly had to make to exit the cab. The wheelbase remained 112 inches and the V-8 engine was still the only one available. This was the last year that Ford pickups would be equipped with steel-spoke wheels.

For Chevrolet, this was an all but forgotten year when it came to pickups. The 1935 models, known as the Chevy EB, came with a standard front bumper and an optional rear bumper. Only 6,192 were produced, including all models, and very few are still around.

1936

Chevrolet introduced hydraulic brakes in its pickups. Until this year, all pickups had used cable-activated mechanical brakes. This year Chevy offered only one pickup model, the first in the "C" series, a line of full-sized pickups that are still manufactured today and still sell close to a half million vehicles annually. It had a half-ton cargo capacity, and a six-foot box. This would be the last year that Chevy pickups would have floorboards and cab door posts made of wood.

This was also the first year that Ford pickups were fitted with artillery-style wheels. In the interest of fuel economy (this was a Depression year remember), Ford offered an alternative to the still-available 85-hp V-8 engine. It was a tiny 136 ci V-8 producing 60 hp. A great loss of muscle came with the diminutive powerplant, however.

Late in the year Ford made four-wheel-drive available for the first time.

For those who wanted a hybrid combination of a truck and a car, Ford manufactured in 1937 a "pickup coupe." The grafting was accomplished by leaving the trunk cover off the coupe and attaching a 33-inch by 64-inch cargo box to the trunk. The concept was a good one, but the methodology didn't work. By 1938 the "pickup coupe" was gone, never to be seen again. The car/truck hybrid returned, however, 20 years later in the form of the Ford Ranchero.

1937

In Chevy pickups, the gas tank was moved under the seat. The passenger's seat had to be removed every time the tank needed feeling. This caused an inconvenience that would last, predictably enough, for only one year. The box was five inches longer than that on the previous year's model. It now measured 77 inches in length. The engine was bigger too: 216.5 cubic inches, up from 208.

Ford's pickups came with a redesigned cab in 1937. The windshield was now divided in the middle by a bar and the front grille became oval-shaped. These trucks came to be known as "barrel-nosed." The cargo box grew by four inches. The wheelbase remained the same and Ford, despite its fallbacks, continued to offer the mini V-8 engine as an economical alternative to the full-sized V-8.

1937 TOP TEN BRANDS OF LIGHT TRUCK

	BRAND	NUMBER SOLD
1	Ford	189,376
2	Chevrolet	183,674
3	International	76,174
4	Dodge	64,098
5	GMC	43,522
6	Plymouth	13,709
7	Diamond T	8,118
8	White	5,933
9	Mack	5,513
10	Studebaker	5,129

This 1975 Chevy Custom Deluxe has been equipped with a chrome tool box.

This 1965 GMC Sportside pickup is being used by a small race track to transport racing fuel.

Closeup of rear metal gun racks. Many sportsmen prefer to carry their fishing poles and umbrellas on their gun racks when not hunting.

This 1989 Chevy S-10 is used by an auto parts store as a delivery vehicle.

Rear view of a 1994 Ford Ranger bed.

The 1994 Ford Ranger can be customized
with a fiberglass camper shell.

1939

Chevrolet pickups came with a totally different cab in 1939. The split vee windshield cranked open at the bottom for fresh air. The grille had a chrome rib cage design and the cab was roomier. This design remained fundamentally unchanged for the next eight years. The changes worked as Chevy pickups rose in popularity and, in 1939, for the first time out sold their Ford counterparts.

By 1939 Ford was offering options on their pickups that included four-wheel drive, a heater, a sliding rear window, heavy-duty clutch, over-sized tires, oil bath air cleaner and road lamps.

were now mounted at the bottom. In an odd style change, the rear window was smaller now than it had been the year before, which caused an annoying shrinkage in rear visability for the driver. Wheelbase: 112 inches. Suspension: Transverse spring. Standard engine: 221 ci V-8, 85 hp. Optional engines: 239 ci V-8, 95 hp (rare); 136 ci V-8, 60 hp (the Depression-special ecomony engine still lacked the power to haul much of anything).

The 1940 Chevy pickup was almost identical to the 1939 version, except that the box was three inches longer and one inch wider. That may not sound like much, but the result was two cubic feet of additional loading space. The boxes were stronger too, as a heavier-gauge steel was used. The canopy to cover the box was still offered as an option but was rarely ordered.

1940

After a few years of having their own individual styling, Ford pickups once again took on the look of their passenger car counterparts. The seam between the cab cowl and the roof was gone, as this piece was now a single stamping. The windshield no longer cranked open for ventilation. The windshield wipers, formerly mounted out of neccesity at the top of the windshield,

1941

The 1941 Chevy pickup had a dramatically different look. This was the first of Chevy's Art Deco series. The truck now boasted a lavish chromium ribbed grille, flat-topped front bumpers, and distinctive parking lights piggybacked atop the headlights, each in their own streamlined housings. It was about as modern as

The 1987 Ford F-150!

a truck could look in 1941, and the classic styling led Chevy to a record sales year.

The standard engine in the Ford pickup, which had earned a reputation for running hot, was upgraded in May 1941 from 85 to 90 hp. The optional 95-hp V-8 remained the same. A new option, a six-cylinder, 226 ci engine producing 90 hp became available. The mini-engine economy model option changed from the scaled-down V-8 to a four-cylinder, 120 ci engine that produced only 30 hp and had previously done duty as the powerplant for Ford's smaller tractors. Times were tough.

1942

On December 7, 1942, the Japanese attacked Pearl Harbor and thrust the United States into World War II. Only a small number of civilian Chevy pickups were made in 1942 before production was halted, then redirected toward the war effort. Today, known as blackout

models, the 1942 Chevys are extremely rare. Pickup production didn't resume until mid-1944, and then only in response to a domestic emergency.

Ford halted civilian production in February. During the short time that 1942 models were produced, however, some style changes were evident. The wheelbase grew two inches to 114 inches. The box was three inches wider. The parking lights were now in the front of the fenders while the headlights moved inboard of the fenders. The grille bars became vertical and the front end grew boxier. Plus, to improve the standard Ford engine's overheating problem, the fan was moved to the center of the radiator. The standard engine now came with a three-speed transmission.

1944

Because civilian truck production was stopped by the war, small industries and farmers were struggling with severe transportation problems by 1944. The War

Production Board responded by allowing Chevrolet to make a limited number of civilian trucks. These pickups were toughened up versions of the 1942 model. Available only to qualifying commercial buyers, and only with a four-speed transmission, they came fitted for rugged 6.5 by 16-inch tires.

1945

The Japanese surrendered on August 14, 1945, thus ending World War II. Three days later Chevrolet's defense contract expired and by August 20, production of civilian trucks was back in full swing. The 1945 Chevys were identical to the 1942 models, once again minus the four-speed transmission and oversized tires.

Ford, on the other hand, had been producing civilian trucks since May. Like the Chevys, the Fords appeared near identical to their 1942 models. But, unlike Chevy, who had simply picked up where they had left off, Ford incorporated improvements discovered during the war into their new civilian truck. The advertisements for the '45 pickup boasted "32 Basic Advancements." These included an optional engine that was the strongest yet offered by Ford: the Model 59. It was a 239 ci V-8 producing 100 hp. With Model 59 under the hood, serious hauling and towing became a breeze.

1946

Chevy added some improvements to its pickup in 1946, including stronger fenders that wouldn't crack, six-ply tires replacing four-ply, redesigned transmission bearings, synthetic rubber pump seals and improved windshield sealing. This would be the last year that the Chevy pickup would have the Art Deco styling.

1947

Chevrolet introduced its brand new Advanced Design Series of pickups in 1947, and today these trucks remain a favorite among collectors. Options included a panoramic-windowed deluxe cab. And the addition of rear-quarter windows not only provided an attractive styling element but it also made for a safer truck as the windows eliminated a blind spot. Once the new design was introduced it stayed exactly the same until 1955. Well, almost exactly. Up until 1950 there weren't any vent windows. From 1951-55, there were. And from 1951-53 there was no chrome trim, because of the war in Korea.

1948

Ford put out its new line of "Bonus Built" trucks, to quote their ads. It was the biggest new line of Ford trucks in their history. The trucks ranged from half-ton trucks (F-1) to three-ton trucks (F-8). Magazine ads bragged of the new pickups' "Million Dollar Cab," and it wasn't false advertising either as Ford had shelled out $1,000,000 to design it. The new cab also featured "Level Action Cab Suspension" with insulated mounts in the front, rubber bushings in the rear, and an anchoring system to dampen engine vibrations. The windshield and back window grew larger. The cab had increased headroom, was seven inches wider, sat three men comfortably side by side, had an adjustable seat that slid forward and backward to adjust to the driver's height, and reclined a bit for a more relaxed posture. With the baby boom in full swing, even the cabs of America's trucks needed to be accommodating to romance. The new line proved so successful that it remained all but unchanged until 1951.

1951

Ford's first style change in their pickups in three years came in January. Indeed, the new truck could have been the ugliest pickup in automotive history. Gone were the horizontal grille bars and in their place was this gaping mouth with three horrible teeth (or five if you counted the headlights which were mounted to the ends of the dental stucture). The protrusions were called "Dagmars," probably after the buxom TV personality. With options the cab, on the other hand, was even more luxurious than the "Living Room Comfort" that had been available in the 1948 cab. With the "5-Star Extra" package, the cab came with additional foam rubber padding in the seat and additional soundproofing. In the rear, Ford removed the steel flooring in its boxes. Now the floors were wood with steel skid strips. Improving fuel economy without sacrificing power was the job of the new "Power Pilot" which governed the engine depending on how much cargo the truck was carrying.

This 1986 Ford Ranger has been put to work towing a trailer containing a Legend race car.

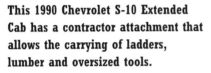

This 1990 Chevrolet S-10 Extended Cab has a contractor attachment that allows the carrying of ladders, lumber and oversized tools.

This after-market product is known as a Fold-N-Haul. It attaches to the rear of a truck like a trailer hitch and is used to carry recreational vehicles—motorcycles and bicycles—as well as hunting equipment and animals.

1952

Ford debuted a brand new standard six-cylinder engine for its pickups. This was also the first year that Ford made its first engine with overhead valves. It was a 215 ci engine that produced 101 hp. The V-8 engine option also got pumped up to 106 hp.

1953

The Ford Motor Company celebrated its 50th anniversary and their present to America was the F-100 truck, which has been called the most-attractive pickup ever. There was a new larger, curved windshield that not only looked great but increased driver visibility by 55 percent. The visibility in the back was also better due to a four-foot-wide rear window. The cab was wider, now measuring 60.7 inches from door to door and there was 36.1 inches of headroom. The seat was 56.7 inches wide, easily big enough to seat three. The engines available in the 1953 model, however, remained the same as those in 1952. An automatic transmission became optional in Ford's lighter trucks. Manual transmission options included a synchromesh three-speed, a three-speed with overdrive and a four-speed. Inside the cab, luxury items available were dual armrests, twin horns, an illuminated cigar lighter, a dome light and dual sun visors.

1954

Ford put a new V-8 engine in it's 1954 pickups. The new "Y" block overhead valve powerplant displaced 239 cubic inches and pumped out 130 hp. The six-cylinder engines were new as well. They now displaced 223 cubic inches and developed 115 hp. The seat upholstery in the new trucks was now made of woven vinyl, stuff meant to last. Other options included a side-mounted spare tire, four-leaf auxiliary rear springs and power brakes.

1955

For the first time since 1947, Chevrolet introduced a new line of pickup trucks. Their now-aged "Advanced Design Series" was replaced by the new "Task Force Series." The most notable of these was the 1955 Cameo Carrier, with its new wraparound windshield for maximum visibility, fenders styled directly into the body of the cab and egg-crate-shaped grille. The box was the same as that of the 1954 Advanced Design model, but fiberglass had been added to the sides. This was the first Chevrolet truck without running boards. The step used to climb into the cab was now hidden behind the door. This truck also introduced a new V-8 engine, which soon became known for its durability. The engine was slow to wear because of an enlarged cylinder bore and shortened stroke. The engine also breathed easier than previous Chevy truck powerplants. This was because of a new idea by Edward N. Cole who designed a tremendously simplified valve mechanism. This was also the first Chevy truck to feature open drive, abandoning the closed torque tube driveline that had been used until 1954. The interior of the cab was completely redesigned, the most notable change being an overhanging crown above the dashboard. The new control panel was designed to form a big "v" in front of the steering wheel. One of the options included a radio, dual-ashtray combo that was mounted to the center of the dash. Swingout ashtrays on either side of the radio offered both the driver and the passenger a comfortable place to flick.

Ford replaced their tube-type tires on their F-100 model with tubeless tires in 1955. In the meantime, both the eight- and six-cylinder Ford truck engines were given more power. The Y-block V-8's power was boosted to 132 hp and the I-6 engine was strengthened to 118 hp. Inside the cab, a key switch rather than a push button activated the starter. On the F-250 series, power brakes became an option. In 1955, a record number of Ford trucks (all series) were sold. Ford sold 373,897 trucks in 1955, breaking the old Ford record set in 1929.

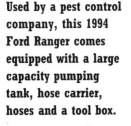

Used by a pest control company, this 1994 Ford Ranger comes equipped with a large capacity pumping tank, hose carrier, hoses and a tool box.

The 1987 Chevrolet C-20 Utility model.

Used in desert and cross-country racing, this 1990 Ford Ranger Off Road Racing Truck is equipped with four-wheel drive, brush catcher, fog lamps, safety roll bars, emergency tool kit, rally package and racing instrument panel.

MID-1950s F-100 PICKUP PRODUCTION FIGURES

1953:	116,437
1954:	101,202
1955:	124,842
1956:	137,581

1956

Safety became a factor for Ford trucks in 1956, and a couple of the changes made in Ford's pickups were designed to make the trucks safer. They were: a deeply dished steering wheel designed to help prevent chest injuries for the driver in case of a head-on crash; and interlocking door latches, less likely to inadvertently pop open in a crash. In 1956 Ford trucks also changed from a six-volt to a 12-volt electrical system, which meant the trucks were a lot easier to start. This proved to be especially true in models equipped with a V-8 engine. The F-100 trucks received a longer pickup bed (eight feet) and smaller wheels (15 inches, replacing the old 16-inch rims). The standard tire size now for the F-100 was 6.70 X 15. Because of the larger cargo box, F-100 trucks now had to be fitted to frames originally built for F-250s.

1957

Ford issued a new line of trucks in 1957. The new trucks, with their squared-off styling, looked very modern at the time. The separate fenders, running boards and high-crowned hood were gone. The cab and box was now a single unit, just as Ford cars had looked for some time. The height of the new pickups was lowered by three and a half inches. The hood covered the tops of the front fenders. The flat hood gave the driver additional visibility. As Chevrolet had done in 1955, Ford trucks now had an inboard step hidden by the doors, replacing the old running boards. Two of Ford's most popular pickups this year were the new Ranchero and the wide-box Styleside. Ford was ahead of Chevy when it came to wide boxes. Unlike Chevy, Ford now put the wheel housings inside the cargo area and opened up the cargo area to nearly the box's full width. The Styleside box boasted 45 percent more load space. For additional ease in loading and unloading the Styleside, the tailgate was made wider too. It now measured 50.2 inches. Inside the cab, Ford advertisements bragged of the new "Driverized" environ. The air vents were now mounted on top of the cowl. There was a full 59 inches of shoulder room and the seat width had grown to 63 1/8 inches. The windshield was 61 1/2 inches and offered a panoramic view. A wide, panoramic rear window became optional. More changes were made with safety in mind. Ford trucks now had double-grip doorlocks, rearview mirrors and a padded dashboard. On the F-100 model, both a six and a half foot and eight-foot box were available. Most preferred the bigger box, as the six and a half foot box looked stubby on the F-100 due to its new styling. The big Ford pickup, the F-350, now came with a nine-foot box. The engines in the new Ford trucks were the 223 ci I-block six-

cylinder (139 hp) and the 272 ci Y-block V-8 (172 hp). Ford-authorized extra-cost items now included: Chrome front and rear bumpers, heavy-duty radiator, bright metal hub caps, front tow hooks, eleven-inch clutch, four-speed synchromesh transmission, grille guard, outside rearview mirror, windshield washers and, what a great idea, an electric shaver!

The '57 Chevy trucks were distinguishable from their predecessors in the Task Force Series by a new grille. The grille was shaped like a large trapezoid with a small trapezoid inside. The hood was also flatter and sported twin "windsplit" bulges.

Ford introduced its bold new Ranchero pickup in 1957, the first vehicle in 20 years to be a full-fledged hybrid of car and truck. The idea, which would be repeated by Chevrolet a few years later in the form of the El Camino, was to combine pickup utility with car style. The 1957 Ranchero, for example, was the only pickup truck produced that year to have independent front suspension. Every other truck on the market had a solid front axle. This meant that, for a hauling machine, the Ranchero handled with incredible ease. There were other exclusives and firsts as well. The Ranchero was the first light truck to offer air conditioning as an in-dash unit. There was a choice of four engines, so large for the weight of the vehicle, that Rancheros instantly became popular as towing vehicles at drag strips. The

engines were a 223 ci six-cylinder, as well as three eight-cylinders, measuring 223, 272 and 312 cubic inches of displacement respectively. The Ranchero was basically a Ford station wagon (usually a Del Rio or a Ranch Wagon) with the top of the cargo section removed. To save in costs of production, the box floor was laid right over a station wagon floor pan. This arrangement turned out to be a problem early on as rain water that gathered in the box would leak down into the car's understructure. Like all of Ford's vehicles in 1957, the Ranchero was designed to look long. It even had tail fins that went from the door handles to the end of the box, forming spears above the truck's cone-shaped taillights. The Ranchero had luxury options that were really luxurious when compared to the options on other trucks. With the Ranchero, a buyer willing to spend the money could get power windows, power adjustable seat, power brakes, power steering and automatic transmission. One problem with the early Rancheros involved the wraparound windshield, which tended to cause a glare problem from the sun that made the dashboard unreadable. To solve this problem, Ford built above the dashboard a sun visor. The 1957 Ranchero could handle a payload of 1,190 pounds. Since the tailgate lowered to a position that was flush to the floor of the box, lowering it could effectively expand the box from six to eight feet.

1958

Chevrolet discontinued production of its Cameo Carrier model in February after producing only 1,405 of them, making the 1958 Cameo Carrier one of the rarest pickups around. The Cameo had been considered the most glamourous pickup in the world during the three-plus years of existence, but it wasn't that much different from Chevy's other deluxe stepside pickups. The difference was customization. The Cameo had custom taillights, full wheel covers, a fancy rear bumper and a hidden fibreglass spare-tire carrier.

Following Ford's lead, who introduced the wide-box pickup in 1957, and to replace the Cameo Carrier, Chevy announced three new Fleetside pickups featuring six-and-a-half and eight-foot beds, double-wall side construction and an extra-wide tailgate. It also had corrosion-proof, nonshed hardwood floors. The Fleetside differed from the Cameo in that its box was metallic and the tailgate was almost as wide as the box, making cargo easier to unload. Also making its debut was four-wheel drive, then available for the first time on all of Chevrolet's half-ton, three-quarter-ton and one-ton chassis. To give the driver improved night visibility Chevy introduced quad headlights on its 1958 pickups. To make room for the extra lights, the front fenders had to be redesigned. The grille in the new trucks now crossed the entire front of the truck. Imbedded in the grille were rectangular parking lights.

Though the 1958 Ford trucks are virtually identical to their 1957 counterparts, there were a couple of subtle changes. Single headlights had been replaced by quad-headlights. And, half way through the year, a bigger and more powerful engine was introduced. The 292 ci V-8 could now produce 186 hp.

The Ford Ranchero car/truck hybrid came with a series of new engine options in 1958. Tops among the options was a whopping 300 hp 352 ci eight-cylinder powerplant that required high-octane fuel. The 332 ci V8 was another new option. This engine came in two versions, one capable of 240 hp and the other 265 hp.

1959

The 1959 Ford trucks were again very similar to the previous year's models. The formerly round parking lights were now rectangular and there were several other minor styling changes, but the big news was that

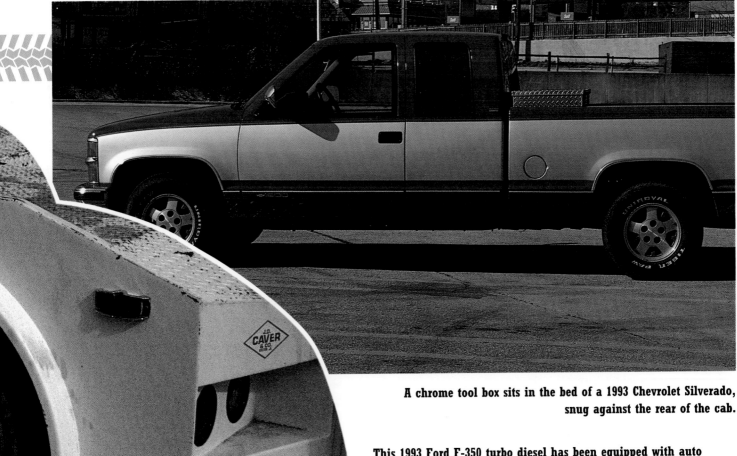

A chrome tool box sits in the bed of a 1993 Chevrolet Silverado, snug against the rear of the cab.

This 1993 Ford F-350 turbo diesel has been equipped with auto transport bed, front guard rails, bug deflector and side rails.

The 1994 Ford F-150 Extra Cab with camper shell attached.

Ford, for the first time, was offering four-wheel drive in their larger pickups. Four-wheel drive would not become available in Ford's lighter trucks for another 15 years.

Following the lead of Ford's Ranchero, Chevy produced their own car/truck hybrid, the El Camino. It was the most intense blend of pickup utility with passenger car design ever seen.

The 1959 Chevy passenger cars were futuristic in design, and the El Camino absorbed many of these features, mostly from the Bel Air. It had thin roof pillars, thin air scoops at the front of the hood, and big fins at the rear. Despite the fact that the cabin was basically that of a passenger car, the El Camino was fitted with a cargo box that was 6 1/4 feet long, 5 1/4 feet wide and 12 3/4 inches high, making 32 1/2 cubic feet in cargo space.

The El Camino had the room to carry a lot of stuff, but did it have the strength to haul it? That was another question. The maximum load for an El Camino was only 1200 pounds, and even that weight was only haulable if you bought into several options such as the oversized tires (8.5 X 14) and the heavy-duty rear springs.

Loading and unloading an El Camino could be a problem as well. The tailgate was only four feet wide, so anything wider than that was awkward to get in and out of the box.

The original El Camino came in two models. One came with a six-cylinder 235 ci engine generating 135 hp, and the other had a V-8 powerplant available both in 290 hp and 335 hp versions. Here was a car/truck hybrid that could really show off.

The standard transmission for the El Camino was a column shift three-speed. Options included a three-speed with overdrive, a four-speed that came from a Corvette and two different types of automatic.

Folks expected the inside of the El Camino's cab to reflect it's hybrid nature, but this was not the case. The cockpit was truck all the way, with the emphasis on convenience rather than glamour. Only by paying for many of the available options could the El Camino's interior be given the glitz befitting its Bel Air-ish exterior.

The El Camino was not initially popular. Chevy brought the hybrid back for a second crack at success in 1960, but sales once again were not spectacular. At that point the El Camino was put on hiatus until 1964, when it made a comeback.

Over at Ford, the El Camino's predessesor went through some changes in 1959 as well. Because Ford placed all of its cars on the same wheelbase in 1959, and the Ranchero was mounted on a car wheelbase, Ford's car/truck hybrid grew by two inches. The extra room came in the form of a longer box.

1960

It was the jet age, so Chevy ushered in a whole new era of pickups in 1960 by incorporating jet designing in its trucks. At the front of the trucks, above the quad headlights, were "cat's eye" pods, designed to resemble the intake manifold of a jet fighter. The trucks were lower, longer and wider. In fact they stood a full seven inches lower than their 1959 ancestors. The lowering was done by altering the frame to fit a drop-center cross-member, and by flattening out the roof of the cab. Despite the fact that the trucks were lower, there was actually more headroom inside the cab, almost one and a half inches of additional headroom.

The cab was wider so that three could sit in the front

more comfortably than ever. The lowering, widening and lengthening afforded the new trucks more cargo room, a wider load capacity, and improved cornering and handling.

Despite all of the other changes, the powerplants that went under the hoods of the 1960 trucks remained the same as those that had been in the 1959 models.

This was also the year that Chevrolet first put independent front suspension in its trucks. The suspension was achieved by using rugged torsion bars instead of the old beam axle.

It would be another six years before Ford put independent front suspension in its pickups.

The United States Air Force and Navy ordered 3,482 pickup trucks from Ford. In the meantime, Studebaker entered the pickup fray with "The Champ", whose interior looked like that of a passenger car but whose reinforced frame gave it truck strength.

By 1960, Ford's squared-off truck look, so modern-looking in 1957, looked terribly dated—and this was the last year that the "refrigerator" look would be in place.

In October 1960, Ford introduced the new Econoline pickup truck, a truck that was obviously very different from all other pickups. You could tell from the first glance. That's because the engine was actually inside the cab and the front seat was at the very front of the vehicle, like a city bus. This "cab-forward" design offered the driver an unobstructed view—although many drivers complained that the new perspective took some getting used to. The Econoline ran on a newly designed 144 cubic inch, six-cylinder engine. Its box was seven feet long, 22 4/5 inches high, and 49 inches wide at the tailgate (48 inches at the wheel housings). The new truck was very good at hauling large objects, but not so great at carrying around the heavy ones. The half-ton truck had only a 1650-pound payload. Other than the placement of the engine, the Econoline was also peculiar because its front shock absorber mounting points were unusually high in the wheel wells. The new truck proved to be popular with the Pentagon, who purchased them up as transport vehicles. Though funny looking, the Econoline proved popular enough to stay in production for eight years.

The first Econolines were certainly not built for luxury. They were designed to be small-business delivery vehicles so most items of convenience were not in-

This 1992 Chevrolet 1500 Sport Model has a special 454 ci motor under the hood.

cluded. There was no passenger seat, for example—although a swing-away passenger seat was optional. Even the heater and the radio were extras. The Econoline was also the last vehicle in American automotive history to be produced without an outside lock on the driver's door. Standard on the Econoline until 1962 was a three-speed transmission that wasn't synchronized into first gear.

Ford's Ranchero, which had previously been based on the Del Rio and Ranch Wagon, was based on the smaller Ford Falcon as of 1960. The Ranchero would continue to be based on the Falcon until 1966. Despite the downsizing, the Ranchero had adequate muscle with a payload capacity of 800 pounds. Though the wheelbase shrunk by nine-and-a-half inches, the cargo bed remained six feet long. The new Ranchero had 31 3/5 cubic feet of cargo space. The floor height was 27 inches and the side-loading height was 38 9/10 inches. The entire vehicle was 189 inches long. It got 30 miles per gallon (mpg) with its super-economical 144 ci six-cylinder engineer. The standard transmission was a manual three-speed, with an automatic transmission as optional. The Ranchero in 1960 was the cheapest pickup truck on the market. It was also extremely popular, averaging 20,000 sold per year.

1961

In 1961 Ford trucks had a new look. The boxy refrigerator look was gone, replaced by a truck with softer angles. In other words, the new Ford trucks looked a lot more like the new Ford passenger cars.

The extremely vertical windshield had been replaced by a windshield that canted forward. The windshield was also higher and the rear cab window was 28 percent larger.

The F-series trucks continued to be built with cab and cargo box as one piece. This was thought at the time to be an innovation, but it turned out to be a flaw.

The reason was rust.

In the old days, before 1957, the cab and the cargo box were separate. When the box began to rust, since

A 1990 GMC 1500 King Cab with a protective bed liner.

corrosion was an inevitability in many parts of the country, owners used to pull the old box off and build their own makeshift cargo box, thus extending the life of the cab and the engine.

But now that the cab and cargo box were a single entity, a corroded out box often meant a whole new truck was needed.

There were also reports in 1961 that the Ford Styleside trucks (wide cargo box models) had trouble opening and closing the doors when the cargo box was full.

Engine options for the F-100, F-250 and F-350 trucks were the 223 ci six-cylinder (135 hp) and the 292 cubic-inch V-8 (160 hp).

The standard transmission was a three-speed. New features on the 1961 models included: an "instant action" tailgate latch on all Styleside pickups, hinged support arms replacing chains on the tailgate (Styleside only). On the narrow cargo bed models (Flareside), chains were still used to open the tailgate, but running boards had been added between the cab and the rear fenders to make loading and unloading the cargo box easier.

Four-wheel drive remained available on the F-100 and F-250 models but only those with the Flareside narrow cargo box. The 4X4 models were built only on a special 120-inch wheelbase. The front grille consisted of two long horizontal bars.

1962

After the massive changes that led to the 1961 pickups, Ford remained pat in 1962, changing very little. The cab and the box remained integral. Base cost of a 1962 Ford pickup: $1,939.

The cat's eye pods, a fixture on the front of Chevy pickups since 1960, were gone in the 1962 models. The quad headlights were gone as well, replaced by single headlights which were mounted in large oval housings.

The Ford Econoline cab-forward pickup had a new optional engine in 1962, which meant more muscle. The new powerplant was a 170 ci six-cylinder. The roofs of the Econolines produced during the first half

of 1962 had an annoying habit of noisily drumming up and down at high speeds. To help reduce this problem, the truck's design was changed halfway through the year and reinforced ribs were added to the roof to help keep it still no matter how fast the truck was going.

1963

Perhaps Ford was already starting to figure out that the integral cab/box design they introduced in 1961 was not the great innovation that they had hoped for.

In 1963 Ford gave buyers a choice and trucks with both integral and separate boxes were available. The change was made at the last moment, apparently, as Ford was unprepared to design a new box for its pickups. Instead, the optional separate box turned out to be that made for the 1957-60 Styleside. The old box and the new cab created a clash in styles, but Ford still charged extra for this option.

The two long horizontal bars that had comprised the grille in 1961-62 on Ford pickups had now been replaced by six rows of short bars. The trucks also featured Ford's new fully synchronized three-speed transmission, the same transmission that was introduced in Ford's passenger cars that year.

Chevrolet's 1963 light trucks featured headlights that were mounted inside round pods, as opposed to the large oval headlight housings that had been used in the 1962 models.

Chevy also introduced a new coil-spring front suspension in its light trucks, replacing the torsion-bar system that had been used previously.

Chevy's heavier trucks also dropped the torsion bar and returned to the old beam axle and leaf springs. The new trucks received a cheaper ladder frame chassis and the rear suspension was also revamped.

The new rear suspension featured two tight center coils that compressed under a heavy load in combination with looser coils on the outside designed to preserve spring flex.

The engine was new, too. The old stovebelt engine had been replaced by a High Torque six-cylinder with a seven-main bearing crankshaft. Generators were out, alternators were in.

In 1918, Chevrolet sold one truck for every 104 vehicles it sold. By 1963, that ratio was down to one in six.

In 1963, for the first time, Ford's Econoline truck came with a three-speed transmission that was fully synchronized in all forward gears. The standard engine remained the 144 ci six-cylinder that produced 90 hp. Because of the truck's lightweight and modest powerplant, the Econoline offered owners an impressive 27 mpg. Optional in 1963 was a four-speed transmission with column shift and a tough-truck package consisting of the 170 ci engine, 14-inch wheels, a heavy-duty rear axle, stiffer springs and a reinforced frame.

This 1993 GMC Sierra 4X4 pickup is powered by a 350 ci V-8!

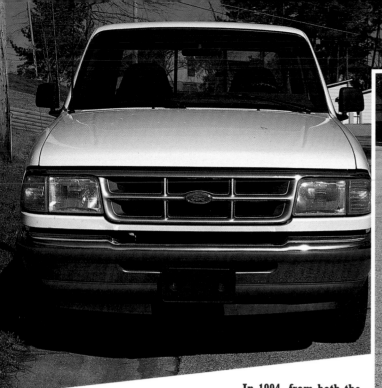

In 1994, from both the front and the rear, Ford's self-advertising was subtle, as is proven by this Ranger.

1964

Chevy made only minor changes in its pickups. The wraparound windshield was gone and in its place was a one-piece slanted windshield. There would be no major style or engineering changes in Chevy trucks until 1967, when the company introduced its Integrated Styling Series.

In 1964 Chevrolet re-introduced the El Camino, the hybrid car-truck that it had first manufactured in 1959-60. This time around the El Camino was based on the Chevelle station wagon rather than the Bel Air, and the marketing department advertised the new version as a personal truck, emphasizing how much fun it was rather than how functional it could be.

The original El Camino had a drab interior designed for work. The new version had the color and the trim suitable for driver and passenger enjoyment.

The El Camino now could be purchased with Chevrolet's hottest engine under the hood, the Corvette engine: a fuel-injected V-8 capable of 360 hp. That's muscle! The El Camino, after all, was not a heavy truck. The lightness of the vehicle make those power numbers even more impressive.

Ford's publicity department didn't exactly boast about it, but the integral cab and box was gone in 1964. Ford returned to building separate boxes to attach to separate truck frames.

The new Styleside boxes for the F-100 and F-250 trucks came in two lengths: six and a half feet and eight feet. The box for the F-350 was nine feet long.

The new tailgates had a center latch, as opposed to the side latches that had been there the previous three years.

Pickups with the short box were still built on a 114-inch frame but the F-100s and F-250s with the eight-foot box were now built on a 128-inch wheelbase, six inches longer than the previous year.

The F-350 truck was built on a 135-inch wheelbase. Making longer trucks was not just a matter of style. The extra length made Ford's pickups better at towing trailers, an increasingly popular American activity in 1964.

The front grille was redesigned. There were now four rows of bars on the grille instead of six, and the bars themselves were fatter than before.

A new optional truck engine in 1964 was a 262 ci six-cylinder, which claimed to increase power over the previous version without sacrificing fuel mileage.

Unfortunately the new engine was not mated with either overdrive or automatic transmissions, thus decreasing its desirability.

In 1964 Ford produced 458,583 light trucks. This would be the last year that Ford trucks would come with a rigid front axle. In 1965, Ford would put independent front suspension into the pickups for the first time and a whole new era would begin.

1965

Along with the new independent front suspension, Ford also introduced into its trucks in 1965 three new engines. The standard engine was a six-cylinder 240 cubic-incher capable of 150 hp.

The two optional engines were the "Big Six," a six-cylinder, 300 ci that created 208 hp; and a new V-8, 352 ci that created 208 hp.

As for the suspension, Ford was not the first to attempt independent suspension in its light trucks. Chevrolet/GMC and Independent had both attempted it in 1963, but couldn't accomplish it without massive and expensive modifications upon its truck frames.

Ford created the "Twin I Beam" which enabled them to put independent front suspensions on their trucks without having to hike the price.

Each wheel still had its king pin in the new design, but rather than attaching both front wheels to a single axle, each wheel was attached to its own axle stub which ran underneath the frame and were attached to mounting brackets on the bottom of the opposing frame channel. The new suspension made drivers and passengers feel as if they were riding in a car.

The Ford Econoline was available with a more varied list of options in 1965. The new Supervan model gave owners 18 inches of additional cargo room behind the rear wheels. Two new engines were offered as well. The standard engine was now a 200 ci six-cylinder and a 240 ci six-cylinder engine was optional. The 144 ci six-cylinder engine that had been the standard powerplant for the Econoline truck since 1960 was now a thing of the past. Also extinct was the four-speed transmission option. The engine, which until this year had been mounted on cantilever arms, was now mounted on a tubular cross-member. These would be the last major changes in the Econoline until the model was discontinued in 1969.

This six-cylinder 4.0 liter engine is under the hood of a 1994 Ford Ranger.

1966

Power steering became an option on Ford pickups for the first time in 1966 and, on the F-100 and F-250 models, power brakes were also optional. White side-wall tires became an option as well, but, as it turned out, not very many truck owners wanted them. The trucks once again had a new grille. The new design featured one horizontal bar, two spear-shaped openings and two rows of small rectangular cutouts. Many of the changes from the previous year occurred inside the cab. A woven seat covering now appeared, which stayed cooler in the summer. Some cabs looked more like the cockpit of a sports car. The new deluxe Ranger option featured bucket seats that could be ordered in red, black, palomino or beige.

In 1966, Ford sold 553,719 light trucks. Ford's trucks were now so comfortable and so easy to drive that they were being purchased by the thousands by people who didn't need a truck, but rather wanted a truck.

The El Camino, Chevrolet's hot car-truck was already able to lay a patch down Main Street USA when, in 1966, Chevrolet, as an option, put even more power under the hood.

The Ford Ranchero, which had been based on the compact Falcon, was redesigned for the 1966 production year and was now based on a Ford Fairlane. The Fairlane would be the basis for the Ranchero car/truck hybrid until 1972, when the Gran Torino/LTD II body-shell would be used.

The Ranchero had grown almost a foot and the box was now 78 inches long. The vehicle, which now had more rounded lines, had more room up front in the cab, as well. There was increased room behind the seats for storage and the cab had grown three inches wider.

1967

For the first time in six years Ford issued a new line of re-styled trucks. The softer, rounded styling was gone, replaced by a sharper, crisper appearance. The look avoided being trendy and lasted, with minor changes here and there, for the next 13 years. The wraparound windshield had been replaced by a curved piece of glass. The sweeps at the rear of the wheel housings were gone completely. In terms of size, power and comfort, Ford's trucks were now so varied that there was one to please just about anybody.

The major changes in the 1967 trucks for Ford weren't cosmetic and they weren't considered major selling points, but they were very important nonetheless.

These changes had to do with safety.

Whereas formerly a failing brake system could turn a pickup truck into a deathtrap, Ford now put a dual hydraulic braking system in its trucks. If a brake line ruptured or a wheel cylinder gave out, the backup system would kick in and it would still be possible to stop the truck. Safety belts and emergency flashers now became standard. The Twin I Beam independent front suspension that had earlier been introduced in Ford's lighter trucks, now became available in their heavy-duty F-350 series as well. The engines remained the same as they had been in 1966. Though Ford still offered the nuts and bolts pickups for folks who needed to haul things from here to there, an ever-increasing amount of time and energy went into pleasing upscale customers through the use of attractive interiors, power steering, air conditioning and bucket seats. This would be the last year that Ford would produce its Econoline model, leaving it temporarily out of the compact truck market.

In 1967, Chevrolet introduced its Integrated Styling Series, in which Chevy's pickup trucks at last offered all of the comforts of a passenger car. The interiors were every bit as comfortable and attractive. All power accessories then available in Chevy cars were available in the trucks. Plus, a wide range in engines and transmissions were available so a truck could be purchased with anything in mind from absolute fuel economy to mountain-climbing.

Four engines were available: 1) a 250 ci six-cylinder; 2) a 292 ci six-cylinder; 3 and 4) a 283- and a 327-ci small-block V-8.

These were some of the last truck engines to be built without the soon-to-be-required emission controls. Transmission options were a three-speed manual, three-speed manual with overdrive, and two different types of automatic transmissions called Chevy Powerglide and GM Turbo Hydra-matic.

The GM automatic proved to be the most popular with buyers since Powerglide had only two forward gear ratios and therefore lacked the Turbo Hydra-matic's smoothness.

Chevy's El Camino truck received new wraparound taillights which could be seen from both the rear and the side.

1968

A Federal law was passed in 1968 requiring that all pickup trucks have side marker lights, so the new Chevy trucks had them added to the front and rear fenders.

This 1993 Chevy Silverado has been customized.

Chevrolet has never been shy when it comes to signing their work.

The grill, split lengthwise down the center by chrome, resembles a brick-laid honeycomb.

The side windows on the 1993 Chevy C1500 are standard. The louvers are custom.

The El Camino received all new styling in 1968. There was a 5.5-inch increase in length. The extra length came in front of the cargo box, however, so hauling capacity remained the same. The cab got three inches taller, a change all but hidden by the new style which gave the car-truck a more streamlined look.

Mazda, slapped the name Courier on it and sold it as a Ford.

The Courier had a 109.5 ci four-cylinder engine producing 74 hp and ran on a four-speed transmission. It would remain part of the Ford lineup until 1982 when Ford again built its own mini-truck, the Ranger.

1969

The sloping hood on Chevy's 1968 trucks was now replaced by a practically vertical front hood edge—a simple change that made a great difference to the truck's appearance. This was the year that Chevrolet debuted the Longhorn, which was basically a long-box Fleetside elongated another six inches. The other new truck model out of Chevy was the Blazer, which took the cab and the box of a short-box Fleetside and combined them into a single unit. The Blazer proved to be one of Chevrolet's most popular trucks of all time, and is still being produced today.

1971

GMC now produced a clone of Chevrolet's El Camino, called the Sprint. The Sprint and the El Camino were identical, with the exception of the nameplates.

1970

The Ranger XLT was Ford's new truck. It was the company's most posh, upscale truck to date. Instead of making a new truck to replace the Econoline compact model, Ford imported a compact pickup made by

A 1995 Chevy S-10.

1972

Ford now offered special packages of options for folks who lived in colder climates. The "Northland Package," offered a truck with a factory-equipped engine block heater, an extra-strong battery and a traction-lock rear axle.

For the first time Chevrolet marketed a small Japanese (Isuzu) pickup truck called LUV. The truck was cheap (average price in 1972: $2,200), it drank very little and it had a 1,190-pound payload rating. The standard engine in the LUV was a four-cylinder, 110 4/5 ci powerplant capable of producing 75 hp. The box, however, was smallish: only six feet long. The width of the box was even more troublesome: 39 inches between the wheel wells.

After six years of being based on the Ford Fairlane, the Ranchero car/truck hybrid was redesigned to be based on the Gran Torino/LTD II.

In 1972 the Ford Ranchero car/truck hybrid changed styles and became based upon the Gran Torino. The powerplants available remained the same, but just about everything else changed. The hood was now very long and the new vehicle sat upon a 118-inch wheelbase. The following year, the second with this design, would turn out to be the Ranchero's most successful. More than 45,000 Rancheros were manufactured in 1973.

1973

Chevrolet manufactured all-new trucks. The four-door Crew Cab and the dual rear wheel Fleetside "Big Dooley" made their debut. This was the last year that Chevrolet offered the economy six-cylinder engine in its popular El Camino trucks, and the first year of the El Camino's new design, which added a solid foot to the length of the vehicle. The car-truck also lost two inches in height, while the wheelbase remained the same: 116 inches. Adding 12 inches to the length without changing the wheelbase length meant that the new vehicle overhung the wheels at both the front and the rear. It wouldn't be until 1978 that this awkward extra length would be chopped off.

Chevy first manufactured its "rounded-line" series of pickups in 1973. These were trucks without right angles. The corners of the windshield and all other windows were rounded, as were the tops of the doors and the rear box corners. These trucks also had larger doors. The doors cut into the roof, thus allowing drivers and passengers to get in and out with greater ease.

There was a problem, however. To make room for the larger doors, the rain gutters had been removed from the roof. When it rained with a window rolled down, water ran directly into the cabin. Chevy tried at first to compensate for its oversight by selling plastic rain gutters that could be attached, but buyers found this a pain and soon the rain gutters were back on the roofs of Chevy trucks.

There were changes to the chassis as well. There were now rear leaf springs, an energy-absorbing steering column that was designed to collapse upon impact, and finned rear-brake drums.

The standard engine remained a 250 ci six-cylinder, but the options had changed. In Chevy's C-20 and C-30 models, one could get a 292 ci six cylinder, or an eight-cylinder displacing either 350 or 454 cubic inches.

Ford revised the styling of its Styleside (wide bed) models. There was now a front-to-rear crease at the level of the side trim spear.

1974

New from Ford was a four-wheel drive option on its F-100 and F-250 series pickups. Ford introduced the Super Cab, which meant that there was now a pickup that could double as a family car—without having the young'uns bouncing around in the cargo box.

SuperCabs came in two styles. One featured a narrow bench that went along the entire width of the cab behind the front seat, enabling the cab to seat six. This bench could fold down so the space at the rear of the cab could be used for storage when nobody had to sit back there. The other style had two jump seats facing one another in the space behind the front seat.

New that year from Chevy was a full-time four-wheel-drive C/K full-sized pickup with a V-8 engine.

Not far into the 1974 production year, Ford scrapped the 250 ci six-cylinder engine for the Ranchero. The standard engine for the remainder of the year was an eight-cylinder 302 ci powerplant.

Here's the 1994 Ford Ranger Splash edition!

This '94 Ranger also has a bed cover.

1975

The El Camino, once so popular, saw that popularity wane in the light of the gas crisis of the mid-seventies that sent gas prices soaring from around forty cents to more than a dollar a gallon. The V-8 engines under the El Camino's hood were thirsty, and they were no longer as powerful as they once had been.

Federal emissions standards took their toll in 1975 on the normally muscular Ford Ranchero, as well. The number of optional engines dropped from six to three. The standard engine became a 351 ci V8. But, because of governmental restrictions, the engine was capable of only 145 hp.

1976

Pickup sales soared. By 1976, three out of every four new trucks was either a pickup or a van. This was also the year that International introduced the Scout Terra, a compact pickup with a 118-inch wheelbase, a 184-inch overall length, 70-inch width, a six-foot box with a 2,400-lb. capacity. The Scout Terra was available with two or four-wheel drive.

1977

Toyota introduced the SR-5 sports pickup, thus bringing that company's number of pickup models to five.

Chevrolet introduced a new one-ton series K30 model. The C10 truck now ran on a 350 V8 diesel engine. All C/K full-sized pickups received a high bucket seat option for the first time.

In 1977, Ford again redesigned their Ranchero car/truck hybrid. The vehicle, formerly based on the intermediate-sized Gran Torino, was now based on the LTD. This gave the vehicle a boxier look. The standard engine was now a 302 ci V-8. Governmental restrictions and a less attractive look had cost the Ranchero

The '94 Ranger, along with many foreign trucks, can be a real head bumper for tall drivers. There may not be as much room inside the cab as there is in some of its competitor's trucks, but no pickup cab is more attractive.

much of its popularity. The vehicle continued to be manufactured, despite diminishing sales, until 1979, when the line was discontinued.

1978

The El Camino was no longer based on the Chevelle, but was now styled after Chevrolet's Malibu line. The awkwardly long styling of the previous model was now reduced by 12 inches. The El Camino was also narrower, but remarkably, despite the decrease in length and width, the interior of the cab and the cargo space remained close to the same. This was the El Camino that, with minor changes, would be produced through 1987.

When the El Camino changed, predictably enough, so did it's twin, the GMC Sprint. GMC's new El Camino-clone was no longer called the Sprint, but took on the new name, Caballero.

Fuel economy was taking a licking at the hands of law makers who had installed clean air requirements on auto makers. To help combat this trend, Chevy in-troduced as an option a 5.7-liter V-8 diesel engine for its C-10 models. Chevrolet's LUV truck, criticized since its introduction in the United States because of its diminutive box, now came with a larger box as an option. Instead of the old six-footer, you could now get a LUV with a 7 1/2-foot box. The payload rating for the LUV increased with this option to 1,650 pounds.

The following year, Dodge entered the efficiency-sized pickup market with a truck designed for sporty performance at play or work. Elsewhere in Michigan, the standard engine for the Ford Courier, the compact truck made by Mazda, was boosted to a 120 ci, 77 hp, four-cylinder.

1980

Volkswagon introduced its first pickup in 1980, but those strange few who might have been looking for a truck with a German flavor were in for a disappointment. The VW pickup was designed and built by Volkswagon of America at its Westmoreland,

This 1992 Chevrolet Silverado Extended Cab has been customized with an after-market paint job.

Pennsylvania plant. Payload: 800 pounds plus. Cost: $7000 for the bare essentials, anything up to $9000 for extras. The truck came in two models, the Plain Jane and the LX, the deluxe model. The LX came with wider wheels, steel-belted radial tires, vent windows and a standard AM/FM radio. Stylewise, the VW pickup was derived from the VW Rabbit. The construction was fully unitized for less weight and a quieter ride. In the front there was independent suspension, rack-and-pinion steering and power-assisted disc brakes. In the rear VW provided a heavy-duty tubular beam axle, leaf springs and self-adjusting drum brakes. The truck came with either a 97 ci gasoline engine or an 89+ ci diesel engine.

1982

Mini-mania!

In 1981, the first American-built mini-truck, the Chevy S-10, hit the roads. By the following year, Detroit was predicting that half of the new pickups sold in three years would be mini-trucks, a shrunken toy-like edition of the classic. Had America's love affair with the pickup soured? Hardly. The problem was gas. The old fashioned pickup truck drank like a fish when compared to domestic and foreign compacts—so the mini-truck was invented. It provided somewhat diminished haulability without costing a fortune at the gas tank. These were some of 1982's most popular minis:

AMC Scrambler. With the 151 ci four-cylinder engine and standard four-speed manual transmission, the Scrambler could get 24 miles to the gallon in the country. Those who went for the optional 258 ci six-cylinder engine got 18.4 mpg. Not bad for an American mini but still thirsty when compared to imports. The bed was only five feet long, whereas most minis went six, but the room was put into the cabin so the Scrambler was a comfortable ride, especially for those who sat in the optional high-backed buckets.

Chevrolet S-10 (GMC S-15) These two models, identical except for their trim, had given birth to the U.S. mini craze the year before, and the S-10 was still setting the standard in luxury and power in its second version. Whereas the average mini-truck struggled when trying to haul anything heftier than a ton the S-10—with

its optional V-6, 110-hp gas engine—pulled two tons without strain. Inside the cabin, the right options (the Sport package) offered drivers the pampering of a limo. It got 24 miles to the gallon without payload. Automatic transmission required. The bed was 89 inches long but the wheel wells stuck up and often interfered with large loads. The independent front suspension, with two-stage leaf springs in the rear, provided a smooth highway ride. In 1983, the S-10/15 was available for the first time in four-wheel drive.

Chevrolet's 1982 LUV built by Isuzu, came with a diesel engine, a standard four-speed transmission, and a 136.6 ci four-cylinder engine. Isuzu marketed this exact same truck as the Isuzu P'UP.

Datsun (Li'l Hustler, Sports, King Cab). Options, options, options. No matter what a customer wanted, Datsun had it. These import minis came with diesel or gas engines, six- or seven-foot bed, wide or narrow wheelbase, recline seats for singles, foldout kids' seats for families, you name it. Halogen headlights made for easier night driving. Variable timing windshield wipers enabled drivers to keep beat with whatever was on the radio. The 2.2-liter four-cylinder gas engine developed 98 hp. The standard transmission was four-speed manual, but options included a five-speed manual with overdrive and an automatic.

Dodge (Ram 50, Rampage). For the first time in 1982, the Ram 50 was made available as either a two-wheel or four-wheel drive. The 4X4 Custom had a 122 ci four-cylinder engine and a four-speed transmission as standard. The 4X4 Sport came with a five-speed transmission and a 155.9 ci engine. These had manual locking hubs and power steering as standard equipment, plus all-terrain tires. With strike and drag angles of 41.5 and 21.5 inches, the Ram 50 earned a reputation for getting there, no matter what obstacles might stand in its path. The Rampage was a Detroit first—a domestic pickup with front-wheel drive. The Rampage

came with McPherson-type Iso-strut front suspension with linkless sway bar, rack-and-pinion steering, angle-mounted rear shocks, power disc brakes, rear load-sensitive proportioning braking system and tinted glass. The problem with the truck was that its bed was too small, just 64 inches long, and it could carry a payload of only 1,140 pounds.

Ford (Ranger and Courier). The Ford Ranger was designed to compete directly with Chevrolet's S-10. Rangers, all built in Louisville, Kentucky, had a big cab with plenty of head and leg room (for a mini, that is). Slots in the bed sidewall accepted 2X4 inserts, thus creating a platform for carrying 4X8 plywood sheets (or the flat payload of your choice) horizontally. Towing limit: 2000 lbs. Double-wall construction of the pickup box and cab roof was standard, as were the "P-metric tires". The tires were a Ford innovation, designed to create eight percent less rolling resistance and improve gas mileage. Another interesting option was a second gas tank holding 13 gallons. When added to the standard 17-gallon tank, it became possible to drive the Ranger more than a thousand miles without visiting a friendly service station.

Like the Chevy LUV, the Ford Courier was actually a Japanese-built vehicle, marketed and distributed by a Detroit company. The Courier was built by Japan's Toyo Kogyo. Like most Japanese-built trucks, the best thing about the Courier was its gas mileage. On the standard 120 ci engine, the truck got 38 mpg on the highway and 27 mpg in stop and go driving. With the 140 ci engine option, hauling a ton of stuff became a breeze. Another option offered a five-speed transmission with overdrive.

The 1994 Ford F-250 Extra Cab Diesel comes with side bed rails.

1980 VW PICKUP
by the numbers

Overall length:	171 inches
Overall width:	64 3/4 inches
Wheelbase length:	103 inches
Cargo box length:	72 inches
Cargo box width:	51 1/4 inches
Cargo box depth:	15 inches
Overall height (at highest point):	56 inches
Road clearance under full load:	4 inches
Curb weight:	1,934 pounds
Standard transmission:	four-speed, floor-mounted manual
Optional transmissions:	five-speed manual; three-speed automatic
Mileage (diesel):	40 mpg, city/53 mpg, highway
Mileage (gas):	23 mpg, city/35 mpg, highway

For easy access to the 1994 Ford F-250 Extra Cab Diesel's cargo bed, there's a convenient chrome step bumper.

This 1987 Dodge Power Ram 4X4 Pickup show truck is equipped with a hydraulic bed, chrome roll bars, custom wheels, custom interior and a chrome tool box.

Mazda (B2000, B2200). The B2000 was the gas model, the B2200 ran on diesel. The B2000 had a 120.2 ci engine, while the B2200—new in 1982—had a 134.8 ci four-cylinder engine that got 32 mpg city and 40 mpg country. The new model had several popular features, including extensive sound-proofing for a quiet ride, expansion-control aluminum pistons and a unique quick-start system that controlled the preheating time of the glow plugs. Both models came with either a six or seven-foot bed, standard five-speed transmission (with no other option) and tinted glass. The trucks looked sharp, too. Rectangular headlights inside a rectangular grille provided a snazzy snout. On the down side, there was no four-wheel drive option and the two-wheel drive lacked the oomph to tow.

Suburu BRAT. BRAT stood for Bi-Drive Recreational All-Terrain Transporter. It resembled some kind of off-road sports car more than a pickup. It didn't carry much and it couldn't tow at all, but it did have a sleek look, a luxurious cabin and four-wheel drive that could get you just about anywhere. Other features included: a four-cylinder horizontally opposed engine, a two-piece combination of T-Top and sunroof, standard Halogen headlights, tilt steering wheel, fully ad-

justable seats and plush cabin fabrics. Plus, the dual-range transmission allowed drivers to switch from front-wheel drive to 4X4 with a flick of the wrist.

In non-mini news: Chevrolet had been offering a diesel engine option on its C-10 models since 1978. Now the diesel powerplant became available for their heavier trucks as well. The new engine was a 6.2-liter V-8, offering the equivalent of 379 cubic inches of displacement. No one offered more engine options on its trucks than Chevrolet.

1983

Nissan—the company formerly known as Datsun—issued a greatly improved version of it's 4X4 Sport Truck. All of the improvements were made with the outdoorsman in mind. This truck was better prepared to go off-road than any previous Nissan. The standard engine was a 2.4-liter two-barrel OHC hemi four-cylinder

options were offered. You could get brush guards and tubular bumpers, a front-mounted electric winch capable of pulling 3,300 pounds, a vinyl tonneau cover for the cargo bed and air conditioning.

The cab was more luxurious than those on previous Nissan trucks as well. This cab offered 38.7 inches in headroom and 43.3 inches in legroom. There was also plenty of room behind the seat for leaning back. The three-way adjustable bucket seats offered special lower-back support, especially comforting for drivers on long trips. One of the niftiest aspects of the new truck was the screened three-position sun roof with removable sun shade.

The truck was not perfect however. Because it had a short wheelbase and a stiff suspension, the ride wasn't as smooth as other 4X4's offered, either on or off-road.

1985

This would be the last year that Jeep would offer their Scrambler pickup. In 1986, the Scrambler would be replaced by Jeep's new mini-truck: the Comanche.

By 1985 nearly one in every three vehicles sold was a truck. All in all 4.6 million trucks were sold.

1986

that delivered 103 hp at 4,800 rpm. This was a major improvement in Nissan's standard powerplant of only two years before, a measly sub-two-liter engine that produced only 90 hp. The new truck's ground clearance was heightened to almost nine inches, perfect for the uncertain paths of the adventurer. The Sport Truck had a wheelbase of a little longer than 100 inches with an overall length just shy of 173 inches. The truck was 66-plus inches wide and 66 inches high. The double-wall cargo bed measured six feet in length, 60 inches in width and 15 1/4 inches in depth. The tailgate opened to both a 90 and a 180-degree angle. The bed stood 32 inches high. The Sport Trucks payload was 1,400 pounds—although 300 of those pounds were an allowance for passengers. The vehicles gross weight was 4,660 pounds. Only one transmission was available, a five-speed overdrive synchromesh manual, known for its smooth shifting. Also standard on the truck were power-assisted brakes (discs in the front and drums in the rear), power steering, tilt-adjustable steering column, tinted window glass and a sliding rear window. The standard tires were the P215/75R-15 steel-belted radials. Mileage was 29 mpg on the highway and 21 mpg under stop and go conditions. Many

Jeep debuted the Comanche, a new mini-truck. It came with either two or four-wheel drive, and had a standard 2.5-liter four-cylinder fuel-injected gas engine producing 117 hp. Options for under the Comanche's hood included a 2.8-liter V-6 engine manufactured by General Motors and capable of producing 110 hp, and an economical 2.1-liter turbocharged diesel engine capable of only 85 hp. The four-speed transmission was standard in the Comanche, with a three-speed automatic as an option. For the diesel engines only there was a five-speed transmission option.

Chevrolet's S-10 trucks received improvements in both of its gas engines. The 2.5-liter four-cylinder standard engine received new lightweight pistons for cooler operation and valve seat changes for more durability. The 2.8-liter V-6 engine, for the first time, was electronically fuel-injected, which both saved money and increased power.

Dodge's Ram series of full-sized pickups received cosmetic changes, including a new grille, headlamp bezels and parking lights, new bumpers, standard tinted glass, steel belted radial tires, stainless steel hubcaps and a new interior trim color: almond.

This 1940 Chevrolet Pickup, on display at a truck show, has been equipped with chrome and brass engine parts, custom wheels and a custom interior.

The Ford Ranger remained the top selling mini-truck made in the United States. In 1986, Ford introduced a new member of the Ranger series, the Super Cab, available both with two- and four-wheel drive.

The Super Cab had a 125-inch wheelbase and added 17 inches behind the passengers' seat for carrying more cargo (or more people).

Also newly standard on the four-wheel-drive Ranger was power steering, gas-pressurized shock absorbers, power brakes and skid plates. The new 2.9-liter V-6 engine offered 20 percent more power than the previous year's 2.8-liter version.

1987

The big news out of AMC's Jeep division in 1987 was the introduction of a short-bed version of the Comanche downsized pickup. The engine was an I-6 capable of 173 hp, which was by far the most powerful engine ever in a small pickup.

Up until 1986 Jeep had been purchasing its I-6 en-

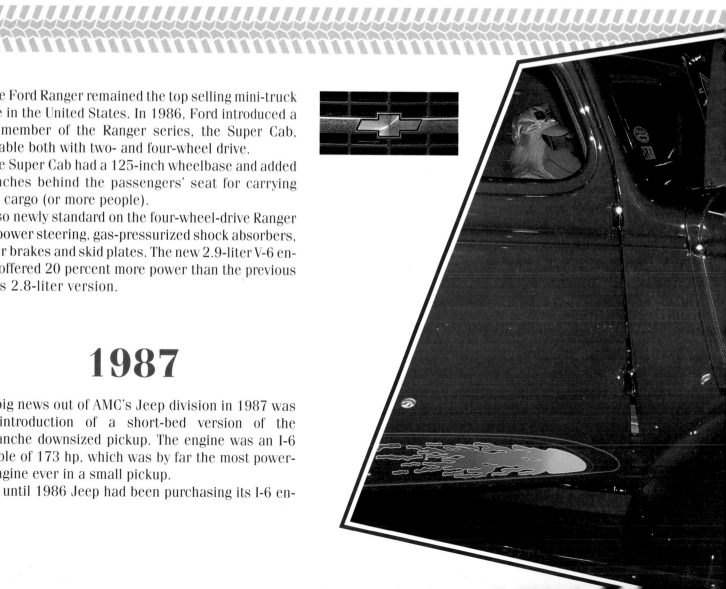

gines for pickups from GM. The change in powerplant translated into a 50 percent increase in get-up-and-go!

The new Comanches could go from 0 to 60 in less than ten seconds. Aware that many pickup owners use their trucks both for long highway trips and for off-road meanderings, Jeep also provided this pickup with a new wide-ratio, four-speed automatic transmission that offered two modes: Power and comfort.

As an option on their four-wheel drive models Jeep offered an "Off-Road Package" that included high-pressure gas shock absorbers in both the front and the rear, a full-sized spare tire, 15 X 7-inch styled wheels, a skid plate package and tow hooks.

Chevrolet made some changes under the hood for its full-sized pickup series. The new engines featured throttle-body fuel injection, making carburetors a thing of the past.

The move to throttle-body fuel injection had earlier been made on Chevy's lighter trucks. The big trucks now had a 350 ci V-8 engine boasting 195 hp.

Chevy's S-10 compact pickups offered a new "Back Country" package that featured a light bridge topped with off-road lights, a brush guard to protect the grille and cradle front fog lamps. A tubular bumper replaced the standard one. A larger generator was also put into the S-10s.

The El Camino also received engine modifications, all made with improved power and fuel economy in mind. There were now roller hydraulic valve lifters for the 4.3-liter V-6 and the 5-liter V-8 optional engine. Properly equipped, the El Camino could now tow up to 5,000 pounds and carry a payload of 1,250 pounds with its 35.5 cubic feet of cargo capacity.

Although Dodge still offered the Mitsubishi built mini-truck, the Ram 50, and still produced a full-line of full-sized pickups, it was their mid-sized truck, the Dakota, that was causing most of the fuss. Though smaller than a full-sized truck, the Dakota still could sit three grown men in the front seat.

It had a trailer towing capacity of 5,500 pounds, could carry payloads up to 2,550 pounds, had a six-and-a-half or eight-foot cargo box, rack-and-pinion steering and a variable rate load sensing proportioning brake valve system.

Over at Subaru, someone finally came to their senses. For years the company had been building BRAT pickup trucks with seats built into the cargo box. You know, just in case someone wanted to sit back there. In 1986, they finally realized that people would rather put cargo than passengers in their cargo bed, and the seats were removed.

Mitsubishi discontinued the diesel option in its pickup trucks. They also restructured the gear shift so that it was no longer necessary to push down on the gearshift in order to get it into reverse.

Mitsubishi's line of trucks featured only three two-wheel drive models: Mighty Max, Mighty Max Sport and the SPX. The first two had the two-liter in-line four-cylinder gas engine capable of 88 hp while the SPX got a larger 2.6-liter engine producing 106 hp.

A five-speed manual transmission was available on all Mitsubishi trucks and three-speeds were optional. Mighty Max featured a double-wall cargo box, dual outside mirrors, tie-down bars, tinted glass, steel-belted radial tires, cargo area light, 18-gallon fuel tank, power assisted front brakes, maintenance-free battery, height-adjustable sport-style steering wheel and full carpeting.

Nissan continued to produce 23 different truck models, the most for any manufacturer, but there were only minor changes in their 1986 models.

1988

Chevrolet issued newly designed trucks. The most noticable visual difference in the new trucks was their slenderness. The sleek look necessitated a small shrinkage in the size of the cargo box, but Chevy compensated by making the box sidewalls suitable for cross braces, enabling haulers to carry a double-decker load.

This 1982 Chevrolet S-10 show truck has a hydraulic bed and a supercharged engine with Nitrous Oxide booster for drag racing!

1990

Until this year changing a tire on a Chevy pickup was a major pain in the butt. The spare was kept in a compartment underneath the box. You had to crawl under the truck, and do brutish work to get the tire out. In 1988, however, Chevy alleviated the problem by installing on their spare carrier a ratchet-handle crank-down mechanism. Turn the crank and the spare lowered itself out of the compartment and onto the ground. (The idea for the crank, it should be noted, came from Isuzu, the Japanese auto manufacturer whose LUV trucks had been distributed by Chevrolet since 1972.)

The new Chevrolet 454 SS (see sidebar) was a high-performance 2X4 that mated the standard C1500 cab with a strong 7.4-liter eight-cylinder engine. With a three-speed automatic transmission and a 3.73 rear axle ratio, the engine produced a maximum of 230 hp.

Also standard for the new model were the 32 millimeter Bilstein gas-filled shock absorbers, a 32 millimeter front stabilizer bar, 12.7 to 1 fast-ratio steering gear assembly and heavy-duty jounce bumpers.

Larger cabs were the order of the day for Dodge. They introduced two new models called Club Cabs. The Dakota Club Cab had a 131-inch wheelbase and the Ram Club Cab had a wheelbase of 149 inches.

The Dakota Club Cab grew 19 inches inside and came with a rear bench seat that could seat three. The Ram Club Cab added 18 inches inside and rear passengers got to sit in two side-facing folding seats.

The Dodge Ram 350 Heavy Duty pickup was equipped with a Cummins Turbo Diesel engine. It was so heavy duty that four wheels weren't enough. It had a double axle in the rear and ran on six wheels!

The 1990 Ford Rangers came with a new more-powerful 4.0-liter V-6 engine that developed 160 hp. It had a towing capacity of 6,300 pounds, up 1,300 pounds from the previous year.

The new engine came only with a four-speed automatic-overdrive transmission, and was available only as an option on the Ranger STX and XLT models. The Ranger SuperCab models got a larger gas tank, growing from 17 to 20 gallons.

Jeep introduced the new Eliminator model which was available both in two-wheel and four-wheel drive models. Each came with either a short or a long bed. Standard features included a three-spoke leather-wrapped steering wheel, wingback seats with cloth upholstery, fog lamps, color-keyed grille, front bumper guards, black body side moldings, power steering, power brakes, a sliding rear window and an upgraded sound system.

1991

Ford's F-series continued to be the most popular pickup in America. Perhaps this was because they were one of the first manufacturers to realize that between a quarter and a third of all new pickup buyers were women. Brand new to their line of trucks in 1991 was a 2X4 Ranger STX that featured cast-aluminum

1990 CHEVROLET 454SS

By the numbers

Engine/Transmission

- Heavy-duty 4.3-liter V-6
- Electronic spark control on the 7.4-liter V-8

Features

- Sport suspension standard
- Tinted glass on all windows
- Deluxe heater
- Front stabilizer bar
- 34-gallon fuel tank
- Halogen headlamps
- Heavy-duty battery (gas models only)

- Cigarette lighter
- AM radio with fixed mast antenna
- Front towing hooks (4 X 4 models only)
- Voltmeter, temperature and oil pressure guages
- Intermittent wipers

Interior/Exterior

- 60/40 seats optional in regular and extended cab models
- Black onyx, catalina blue metallic, crimson red metallic exterior colors
- Garnet interior trim color

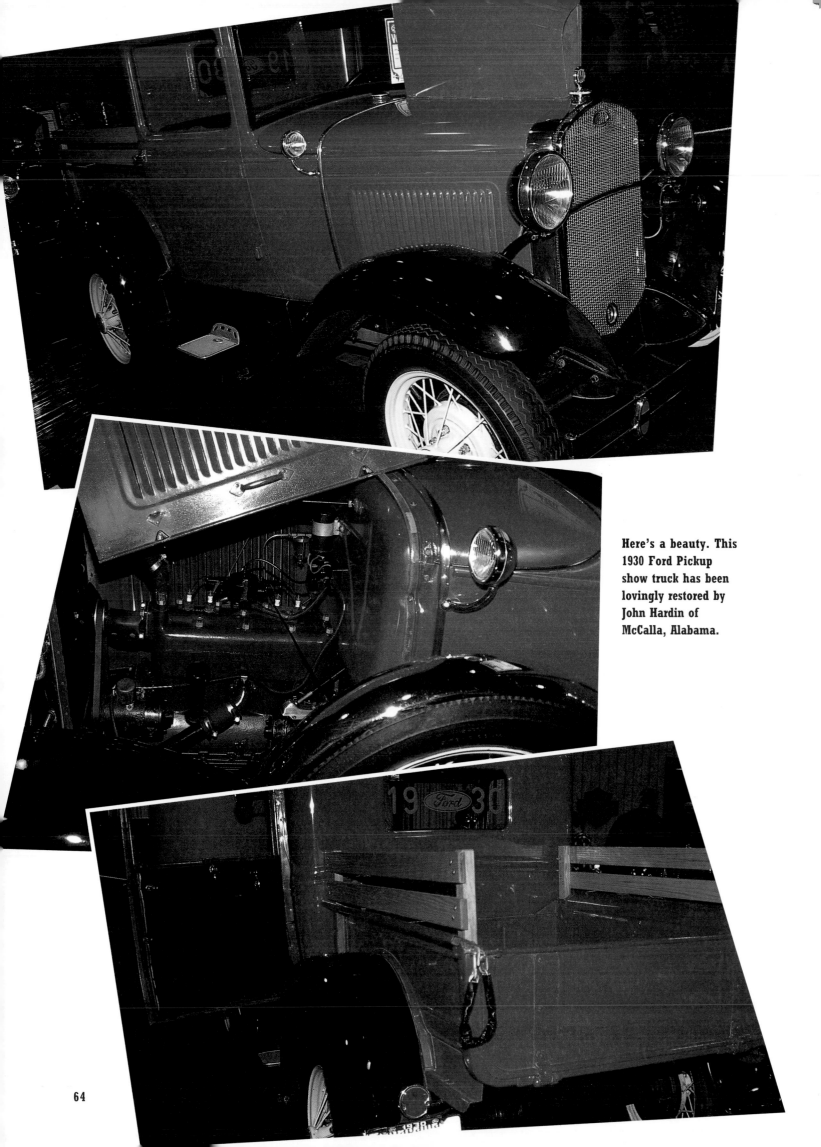

Here's a beauty. This 1930 Ford Pickup show truck has been lovingly restored by John Hardin of McCalla, Alabama.

wheels, heavy-duty pressurized shocks, sport bucket seats, AM/FM sound system, tach, courtesy lights and a leather-covered steering wheel.

There was a more powerful 7.4-liter big block V-8 producing 255 hp in the 1991 full-sized Chevy pickups. Chevrolet/GMC also introduced a new electronically-controlled, heavy-duty four-speed automatic overdrive transmission for their larger pickups. In the S-10 compact pickup, the standard 2.5-liter four-cylinder engine was replaced with a reworked model that was capable of 105 hp.

The Dodge Dakota got a whole new look in 1991 with a new grille, front bumper and aerodynamic headlamps (available only on the LE and Sport models). The Sport 2X4 and 4X4 editions came with a 3.9-liter V-6 with a five-speed manual transmission. The downsized Ram 50, made for Chrysler by Mitsubishi, came with a standard 2.4-liter four cylinder or the optional 3.0-liter six-cylinder.

Jeep's popular pickup, the Comanche, got a boost to its powerplant in 1991. About five hp was added to the standard 2.5-liter four-cylinder, improving its strength to 126 hp. This was done by switching from throttle-body fuel injection to a multi-point system. The two-wheel-drive model has a standard five-speed manual or a four-speed automatic transmission. The 4X4s are reversed, with the five-speed being standard and the automatic transmission being optional.

1993

The 1993 Ranger was lagging behind the competition when it came to roominess inside the cab. The Ranger, along with many of the foreign trucks available, were real head bumpers for tall drivers. There may not have been more room inside the cab, but the room that was there was more attractive. Door trim panels, the steering wheel, seat trim and instrument panel appliques were all new. The standard bench seat now had an armrest, and a state-of-the-art sound system with CD player was available as an option.

The engine was new, too. The '93 Ranger had a 3.0-liter V-6 which cranked out 145 hp. The even more powerful engine, a 4.0-liter V6, was an option for all models.

1990 CHEVROLET S-10 PICKUP

By the numbers

Engine/Transmission

2.5-liter four cylinder engine

- Revised oil system plugs
- Plastic crankcase ventilation hoses
- Plastic evaporative emission pipes
- Closed-bottom charcoal cannister
- One-piece welded design crankshaft pulley and hub
- Polymeric rocker arm cover gasket
- New cylinder head gasket
- Longer engine oil dipstick and tube

2.8-liter V-6, available on two-wheel-drive models only

4.3-liter V-6 engine

- Optional five-speed manual

Features

- Fixed gross vehicle weight rating system
- Bolder instrument cluster
- Lighted vanity mirrors (optional)

Standard Equipment

- Side-view mirrors
- Spare tire carrier
- Side-window defogger
- Door trim panels
- Floor covering
- Grab handle (4 X 4 models only)
- Insulation and sound deadening material

The 350 ci engine came standard in the 1966 Chevrolet Custom Pickup.

The Dodge Ram 50 pickup featured new rear-wheel anti-lock brakes standard. The only engine available was a diminutive 2.4-liter four-cylinder capable of 116 hp. Payload maximum was 1,460 pounds, but could be upped to 2,300 pounds using optional equipment.

Dodge's most popular pickup, the Dakota, made only minor changes for the new season. A new option was a super-strong 5.2-liter Magnum V-8 with the capability to develop 230 hp. The standard engine remained the 2.5-liter four-cylinder. Also available as an option was the six-cylinder, 3.9-liter engine maxing out at 180 hp. The Dakota continued to be available in both the regular cab and super-roomy Club Cab models.

In 1993, Toyota first offered its much-anticipated T100 "intermediate" pickup with three-across seating, a cargo bed large enough for a four-foot by eight-foot panel of plywood and a standard 1,550 payload capacity. All T100s were powered by a 3.0-liter six-cylinder single overhead cam engine that developed a maximum of 150 hp. The standard transmission was five-speed manual. As an option on the two-wheel drive models only, was a four-speed electronically controlled overdrive automatic. The truck also featured rear-wheel ABS, power rack-and-pinion steering on the 2X4s and recirculating ball steering on the 4X4s, and a bed that was 97.8 inches long and 49.2 inches between the wheel wells. The cargo bed was 61.4 inches at its widest. The tailgate could be removed without tools and there were six stake pockets that could be used to provide a duel-tier capacity for cargo.

1994

This was the year that Chevrolet had its severe recall problems with its pickup trucks. Many of the 1994 C/K 10-30 and GMC C/K 15-35 trucks had to be recalled after it was discovered that a brake mechanism had been installed improperly. Because of this, the trucks were showing a nasty habit of losing brake operation. The improper installation also manifested itself as a malfunction of the rear brake lights, a problem that tended to cause rear end accidents.

NEW TRUCKS
They still have that smell

This customized 1995 Chevrolet Silverado comes equipped with an extended cab, a bed cover and custom wheels.

The front of this 1995 Dodge Dakota has been equipped with a bug shield.

This 1995 Dodge Dakota has been customized with after-market high-output lights, perfect for off-road adventures of the nocturnal variety.

The roll bars between the cab and bed of this 1995 Dodge Dakota makes it resemble a racing truck.

You can tell by the 1995 Dodge Dakota Sport's logo that fashion has become more important than function. Instinct tells us that most of these vehicles will never pull up to construction sites with two-by-fours sticking out of the box.

The 1995 Chevrolet Extended Cab C1500 with Z71 package. The Z71 option comes with both off-road equipment and luxury items.

The front end of a 1995 Ford F-150 XLT.

The 1995 Chevrolet S-10 with Extended Cab.

PICKUP LOVE

It's a beautiful thing

It was love at first sight when these two 1990 Chevrolet Short Bed pickups
discovered one another while skinny-dipping in a babbling brook.

TRUCKS AT WORK
Just doin' what they do...

This 1970 Chevrolet pickup is being used by a racetrack to haul and dispense dirt.

This 1988 Ford Ranger is used as a delivery vehicle for NAPA auto parts.

This 1976 Chevrolet El Camino has been souped up into a bracket drag racer!

And some trucks just haul stuff!

This 1995 Chevrolet S-10 is used by a courier company to deliver letters and small packages.

The pickup has allowed the small business person the freedom and mobility to compete with the larger companies. This is a 1986 Chevy S-10, equipped with shell, tools and signs.

Equip a 1987 Chevrolet Silverado with the tow truck package, and you're ready to go hookin'!

MONSTER PICKUPS
Beasts that leap and crush

No, these are not pickup trucks with glandular problems—and, no, they haven't taken too many steroids. These pickups, actually pickup bodies mounted onto special frames, have been converted into the largest and meanest trucks in the world with the help of 66- inch-tall tires and 25" X 36" custom-made steel wheels.

Special tough suspensions made of modified leaf springs and rugged shock absorbers allow these humongous trucks to leap over and crush cars with their power!

This monster truck, now known as "Overtime," started out as a 1990 GMC Sierra.

Bob Chandler's Bigfoot monster truck, the first monster truck ever, started out as a Ford F-150.

Even the most savage beasts started out with a
standard pickup body!

CUSTOMIZED TRUCKS
Low riders in hot colors

The thing to do for a lot of folks when they get a new pickup truck is to customize, customize, customize. Truck owners look at their production model trucks like an artist looks at an empty canvas.

In certain sections of the United States, where the surroundings are urban and the weather is always warm, customization means "slamming," or lowering the pickup truck.

The lower the better.

This is done by cutting down the shocks. The reason the weather has to be warm is that a low rider pickup cannot be driven anywhere near a pot hole. Also, lowering a pickup completely ruins its ability to haul things. But drivers who customize their pickups are into the truck's aesthetics rather than its function.

The interiors of these trucks are usually customized to match whatever flashy paint job has been selected for the exterior. Whatever the customization, the changes are almost always personal expressions of the owner's loves and desires.

Think pink with this 1987 Ford.

This 1989 Chevrolet S-10 answers the question, "How low can you go?"

The cab of this 1956 Ford is so sharp, the owner is considering charging admission!

Guess what company built this 1964 truck?

This 1958 Chevy is red on red. It's about as red as you can get!

Cruise down Main Street in this 1956 Ford
and you'll freeze pedestrians
in their tracks!

RACING TRUCKS

From the back road to the superspeedway

It wasn't long after pickup trucks were invented that folks in the country learned how much fun they were to race down the back roads. These impromptu competitions were run with reckless abandon in a ceremony all too often performed by boys of powerful thirst.

That's how drag racing got started, and pickups were used just as often as roadsters.

Today, pickup trucks are driven by some of the best race car drivers in the world, in trucks that have been carefully prepared by auto racing's greatest engineers.

In 1995, the National Association of Stock Car Auto Racing [NASCAR] announced a new series of races to be called the Super Truck Series. The Super Trucks were a truck body mounted onto a stock car chassis.

Like the stock car, the Super Truck resembled the make and model coming off of the Detroit assembly lines. Already it is obvious that the series will become another battle between Ford and GMC/Chevy.

Chevy S-10s, the GMC C-1500 and the Ford F-150 are currently the favorite trucks to use. The series

It's a race sanctioned by SCCA Racetrucks at the Road Atlanta track in Atlanta, Georgia. That's a 1991 Jeep Comanche in the lead!

takes these trucks to some of the fastest race courses in the world.

The most noticeable difference between a Super Truck and the pickups parked in driveways across America is in the cargo box area. The Super Truck's box is completely covered with sheet metal and has an air spoiler on the tailgate to improve aerodynamics. The trucks are powered with 358 ci engines with a 9 1/2:1 compression ratio. They are limited to a wheelbase of 112 inches. The total truck weighs 3,400 pounds with much of the weight allocations, especially in the cab area, up to the builders. The weight distribution is often determined through wind-tunnel experiments.

One of the first Super Trucks practice races was held as part of NASCAR's Featherlite Southwest Tour Series at the Saugus Speedway in beautiful Santa Clarita, California—the track known as "the place

The cab of this Ford Ranger has all of the safety features of a race car, from a full body harness for the driver to a net-covered driver's side window.

The #55 Ford Ranger SCCA Racetruck. This series used standard compact pickups with no modifications except the shocks, fuel cells and roll cages.

where Los Angeles comes to race." The Speedway is a third of a mile, flat as a pancake, asphalt oval and a stiff test for the handling capabilities of new race trucks. *Stock Car Spectacular* reporter Dave Grayson described it this way in the magazine's March 1995 issue: "Before the trucks were allowed to race they were given a Saugus-style formal introduction. A vehicle loaded with a massive sound system slowly motored its way to the center of the speedway. All of a sudden all of the lights were turned out. The sound system be-

gan playing some funky science-fiction music as bright green laser beams were shot all over the speedway and into the audience. A smoke pot was ignited at the turn-three entrance as the announcer boomed: 'Ladies and gentlemen, the NASCAR Super Trucks!' The trucks came out one at a time and, as they roared around the track, a series of white strobe lights went off to light the way for the drivers and to accent the entire proceedings. The Standing Room Only Saugus crowd stood and cheered.

"The race itself featured four trucks running 25 laps and in a matter of minutes the event settled down to a duel between two Ford trucks being driven by P.J. Jones and Gary Collins. The trucks roared down the straightaways running close to the retaining walls like guided missiles. They handled the flat turns like they were running on rails. In the final laps Collins regained the lead after scraping some paint with Jones. On the final circuit Jones made a last-ditch effort to pass Collins on the ouside only to lose his Ford F-150 in turn three where he parked the back of it into the wall. Collins received the black and white checkers from the honorary flagman, actor James Garner, who was on hand to get a first peek at the new racing trucks."

Watch for them. Super Trucks. They're coming to a track near you!

As you can see by this rear view of the Ford Ranger, race trucks of the SCCA Racetruck Series have open boxes, unlike the trucks of NASCAR's Super Truck Series, whose boxes are covered with sheet metal to improve aerodynamics.

Two 1991 Ford Ranger pickups go nose to tail at 120 mph!

INDEX

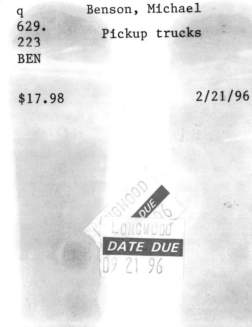

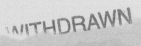